NEW PIANO SERIES

REPERTOIRE ALBUM 1

© Copyright 1994 by The Frederick Harris Music Co., Limited
All Rights Reserved

ISBN 0-88797-416-3

FREDERICK
HARRIS
MUSIC

Official Examination Repertoire of The Royal Conservatory of Music - Grade 1
Répertoire officiel des examens du Royal Conservatory of Music - Niveau 1

NEW PIANO SERIES

The *New Piano Series* is designed to serve the needs of teachers and students, as well as those who play the piano solely for their own enjoyment. Each volume of repertoire comprises a carefully selected and edited grouping of pieces from the Baroque, Classical, Romantic, and 20th-century style periods. Studies Albums present compositions especially suited for building technique as well as musicality. Student Guides and recordings are available to assist in the study and enjoyment of the music.

A Note on Editing

Most Baroque and early Classical composers wrote few dynamics, articulation, or other performance indications in their scores. Interpretation was left up to the performer, with the expectation that the performance practice was understood. In this edition, therefore, most of the dynamics and tempo indications in the Baroque and early Classical pieces have been added by the editors. These editorial markings, including fingering and the execution of ornaments, are intended to be helpful rather than definitive. By the late 18th century, composers for the piano included more performance indications in their scores, a trend which became standard in the 19th century. Therefore, in late Classical and Romantic compositions, as well as in the music of our own time, the performer is able to rely on the composers' own markings to a greater extent.

A Note on Performance Practice

The keyboard instruments of the 17th and early to mid-18th centuries lacked the sustaining power of the modern piano. Consequently, the usual keyboard touch was detached rather than legato. The pianist should assume that a lightly articulated touch is appropriate for the Baroque and early Classical music, unless a different approach is indicated either in the music or in a footnote. Slurs are used to indicate legato notes or short phrases.

Piano Syllabus – RCM Examinations

The Royal Conservatory of Music Piano Syllabus gives full details regarding examinations. Teachers, students, and parents are urged to consult the most recent Syllabus for current examination requirements and procedures.

Le "New Piano Series" a été conçu non seulement pour les professeurs et leurs élèves mais aussi ceux qui jouent du piano pour leur propre plaisir. Chaque album inclus un groupe de pièces de style baroque, classique, romantique et 20ème siècle, soigneusement choisies et editées. Les albums d'étude offrent des compositions particulièrement aptes à développer la technique aussi bien que la musicalité. Les guides d'étude et les enregistrements sont disponibles afin d'aider à l'étude des pièces et pour maximiser le plaisir de les jouer.

Note au sujet de l'édition

La plupart des compositeurs baroques et classiques ne notaient ni nuances ni articulations dans leurs partitions. L'interprète était libre de jouer comme il l'entendait en basant bien sûr son interprétation sur la norme de son époque. Dans cette édition, la majeure partie des nuances et articulations trouvées dans les pièces baroques et classiques ont été ajoutées par les éditeurs. Ces additions, incluant doigtés et ornementation, sont fournies à titre indicatif seulement. A partir de la fin du 18ème siècle, les compositeurs commencèrent à inclure de plus en plus d'indications dans leurs partitions. L'interprète de musique de la fin du classique jusqu'à celles de nos jours peut donc beaucoup plus faire appel aux indications du compositeur.

Note au sujet de l'exécution

Les claviers du 17ème et début du 18ème siècles n'avaient pas le ton soutenu d'un piano moderne. Conséquemment l'articulation était surtout détaché plutôt que legato. Le pianiste devrait donc approcher la musique baroque et début du classique avec une légère articulation à moins qu'une approche différente ne soit indiquée dans la partition ou par une note de l'éditeur. Le legato et de courtes phrases sont indiqués par des liaisons.

Piano Syllabus – Examens du RCM

Le Piano Syllabus du Royal Conservatory of Music contient tous les détails au sujet des examens. Il est impératif pour les professeurs, élèves, et parents de consulter le plus récent Syllabus pour être au courant des pré-requis et des règles des examens.

Repertoire Album 1
TABLE OF CONTENTS

* Canadian composer / Compositeur canadien

HUMORESQUE IN G MAJOR / HUMORESQUE EN SOL MAJEUR

LIST A

Anon.
attributed to / attribué à
Leopold Mozart
(1719 - 1787)

Left-hand notes should be played detached. / On devrait détacher les notes de la main gauche.
The original left-hand part has broken eighth-note octaves. / La partie originale de la main gauche contient des octaves brisées
en croche.
Source: *Notebook for Wolfgang / Album de Wolfgang* (1762)

GERMAN DANCE IN G MAJOR / ALLEMANDE EN SOL MAJEUR
Hob. IX:22, No. 3

LIST A

Franz Joseph Haydn
(1732 - 1809)

Moderato ♩ = 116 - 126

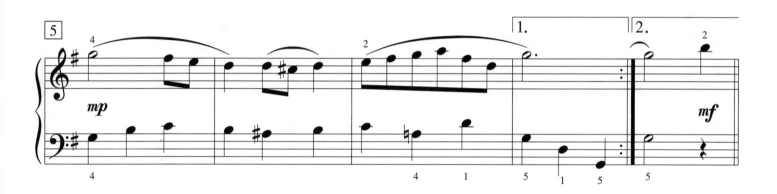

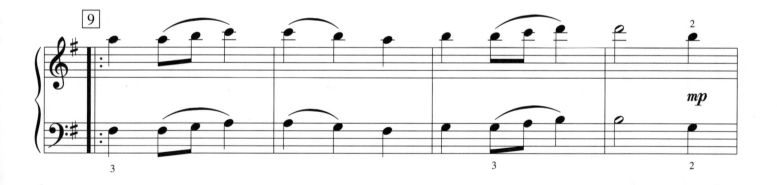

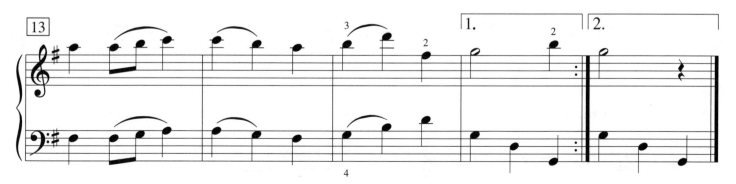

Source: *Ballo Tedescho per il cembalo,* Hob. IX:22

SARABANDE

LIST A

Arcangelo Corelli
(1653 - 1713)

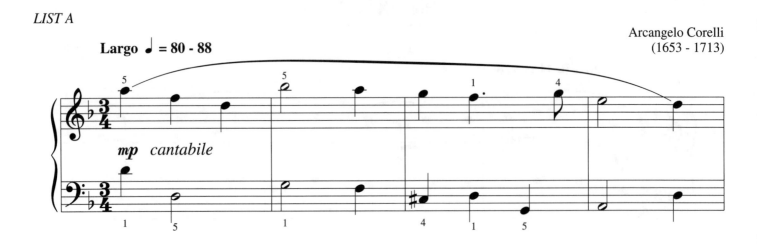

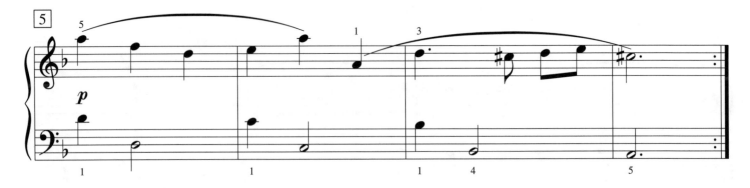

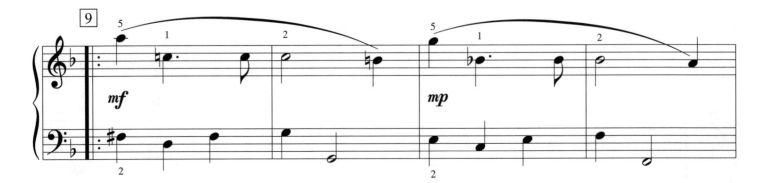

The following ornaments may be added in mm. 4 and 15: / On peut ajouter les ornements suivants aux mesures 4 et 15:

Source: Violin Sonata, Op. 5, No. 7, third movement / Sonate pour violon, op. 5, n° 7, troisième mouvement (1700)

MERRIMENT / LA GAIETÉ

LIST A

Daniel Gottlob Türk
(1750 - 1813)

Vivo ♩ = 104 - 112

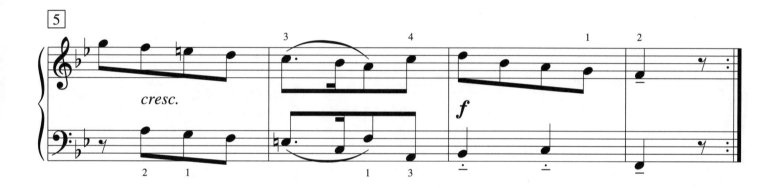

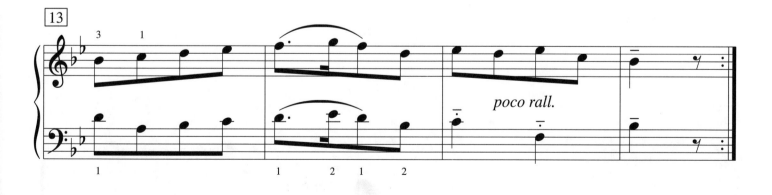

All eighth notes should be played staccato unless marked otherwise. / Toutes les croches doivent être jouées staccato sauf en cas d'indication contraire.
Source: *Handstücke für angehende Klavierspieler* [Pieces for Aspiring Keyboard Players / Pièces pour pianistes débutants], vol. 1 (1792)

ARIA

LIST A

Anon.

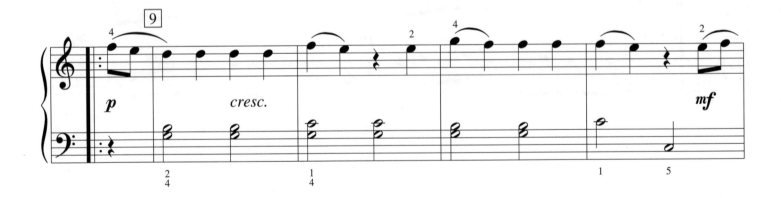

THE HUNTING HORNS AND THE ECHO /
LES CORS DE CHASSE ET L'ÉCHO

LIST A

Daniel Gottlob Türk
(1750 - 1813)

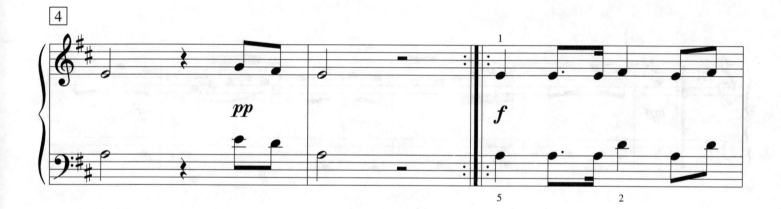

All eighth notes should be played staccato. / Toutes les croches doivent être jouées staccato.
Source: *Handstücke für angehende Klavierspieler* [Pieces for Aspiring Keyboard Players / Pièces pour pianistes débutants], vol. 1 (1792)

CONTREDANSE

LIST A

Anon.

Left-hand quarter notes should be played detached. / On devrait détacher les noires de la main gauche.
All eighth notes should be played staccato. / Toutes les croches doivent être jouées staccato.

MINUET IN F MAJOR / MENUET EN FA MAJEUR
KV 2

LIST A

Wolfgang Amadeus Mozart
(1756 – 1791)

Composed in Salzburg, 1762 / Composée à Salzbourg, 1762
Left-hand notes may be played detached unless marked otherwise. / On peut détacher les notes de la main gauche sauf en cas d'indication contraire.

COUNTRY DANCE IN D MAJOR / DANSE VILLAGEOISE EN RÉ MAJEUR

Hob. IX:22, No. 2

LIST A

Franz Joseph Haydn
(1732 - 1809)

Allegro ma non troppo ♩ = 132 - 144

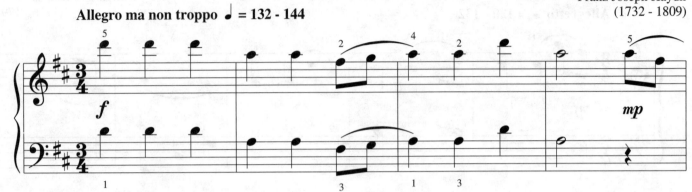

Most quarter notes should be played staccato. / La plupart des noires doivent être jouées staccato.
Source: *Ballo Tedescho per il cembalo*, Hob. IX:22

Recital

BOURRÉE IN A MINOR / BOURRÉE EN LA MINEUR

LIST A

play 2 old ones   Sept 15/95

Johann Sebastian Bach
(1685 - 1750)

Allegro con spirito ♩ = 76 - 80

Source: Partita in B minor for Solo Violin, BWV 1002 / Partita en si mineur pour violon seul, BWV 1002

MINUET IN A MINOR / MENUET EN LA MINEUR

Z. 649

LIST A

Henry Purcell
(1659 - 1695)

Stately / Majestueux ♩ = 112 - 126

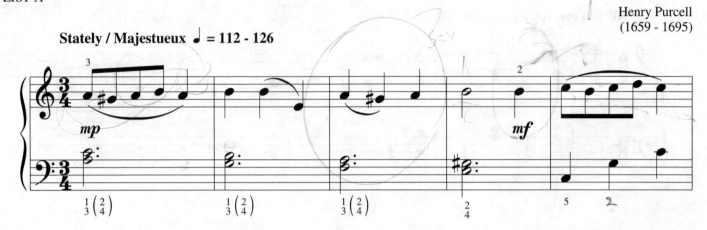

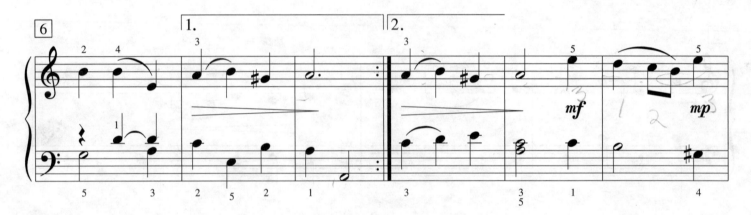

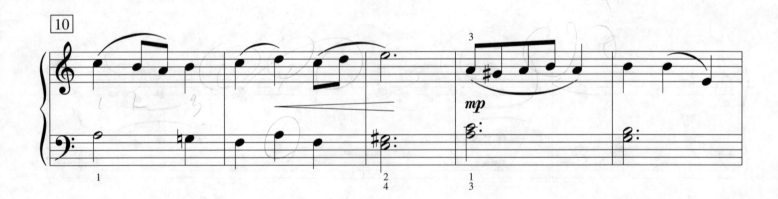

Source: *Twelve Lessons from "Musick's Handmaid,"* Part 2, No. 5 (1689)

Arrangement © copyright 1994 The Frederick Harris Music Co., Limited.

THE JESTER / LE BOUFFON

LIST A

Johann Ludwig Krebs
(1713 - 1780)
arr. Margaret Parsons
(1914 - 1991)

Allegro giocoso ♩ = 76 - 88

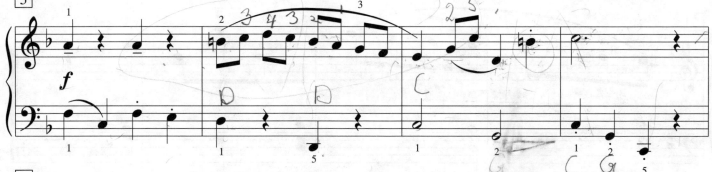

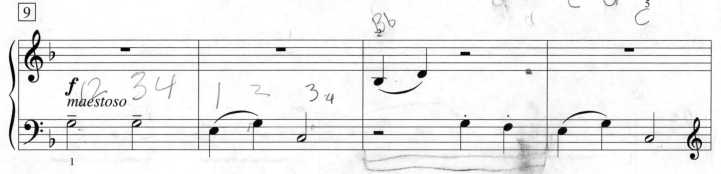

ECOSSAISE

LIST B

Franz Schubert
(1797 - 1828)

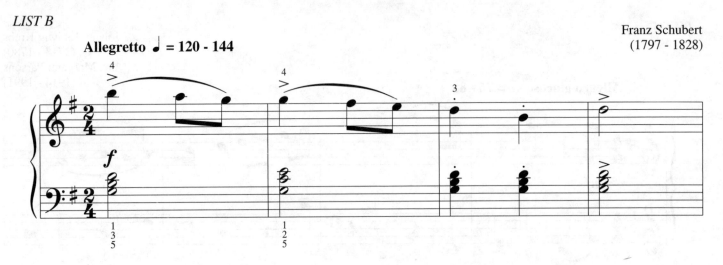

This piece has been simplified. / Ce morceau a été simplifié.
Source: *12 Waltzer, 17 Ländler und 9 Ecossaisen*, Op. 18, D. 145 (*2 Ecossaisen*, D. 618C)

BIG TEDDY, LITTLE TEDDY / GRAND OURSON, PETIT OURSON

LIST B

Linda Niamath
(1939 -   )

Moderately, with warmth /
Modéré, chaleureux ♩ = 126 - 132

Introduction

They waltz together /
Ils valsent ensemble

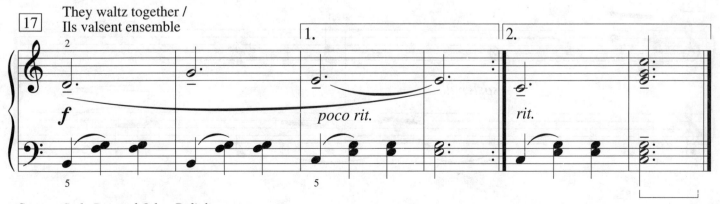

Source: *Soda Pop and Other Delights*

A SAD SONG / UNE CHANSON TRISTE
Op. 36, No. 39

Alexander Gedike
(1877 - 1957)

Source: *60 Easy Piano Pieces for Beginners, Op. 36 / 60 Pièces faciles pour les commençants, op. 36*

DUET FOR ONE / DUO POUR UN

LIST B

Christopher Norton
(1953 -   )

Calmly / Tranquillement ♩ = *ca* **112**

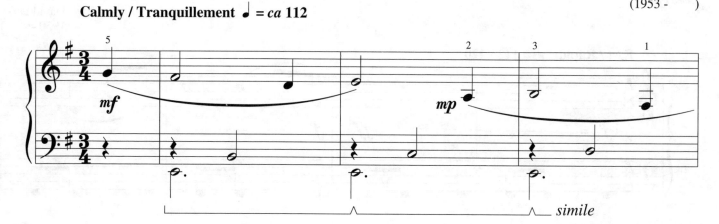

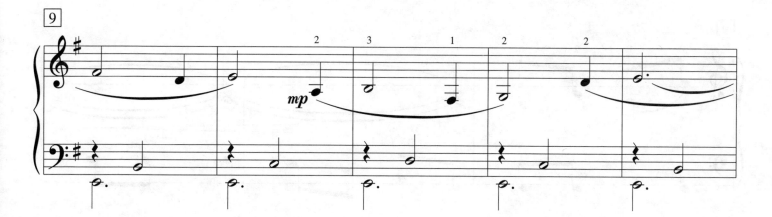

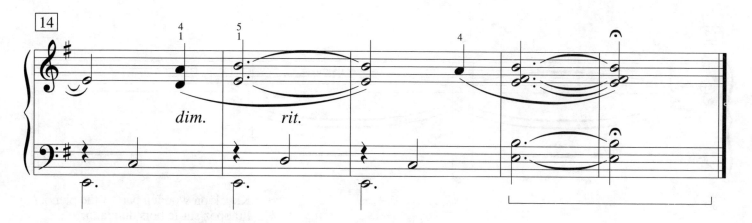

Source: *Microjazz for Starters 2*, No. 6

© Copyright 1990 Boosey & Hawkes Music Publishers Ltd. Used by permission.

MARCH / MARCHE
(Lydian Mode / Mode lydien)

LIST B

David Duke
(1950 -   )

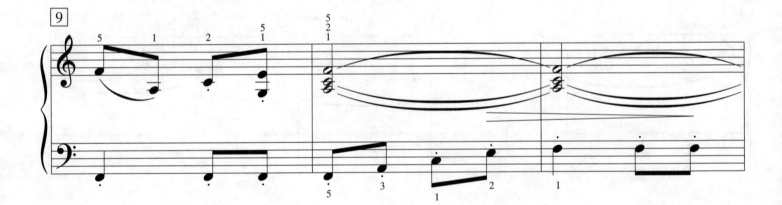

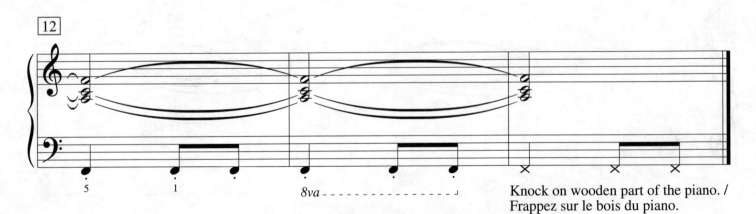

Knock on wooden part of the piano. /
Frappez sur le bois du piano.

Source: *Music of Our Time*, Book 1 / *Musique de notre temps*, livre 1
© Copyright 1977 Waterloo Music Company Limited, Waterloo, Ontario, Canada. Reprinted by permission.

PETITE HIRONDELLE / LITTLE SWALLOW

LIST B

Chanson de danse canadienne-française /
French Canadian dance song
arr. Pierre Gallant
(1950 -   )

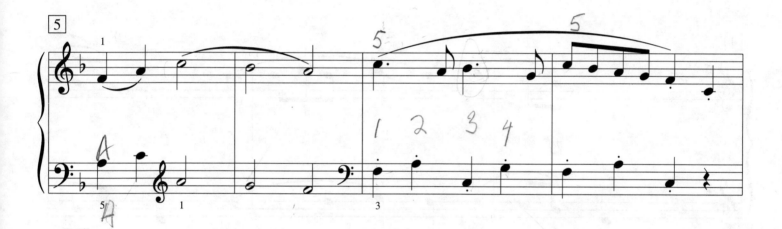

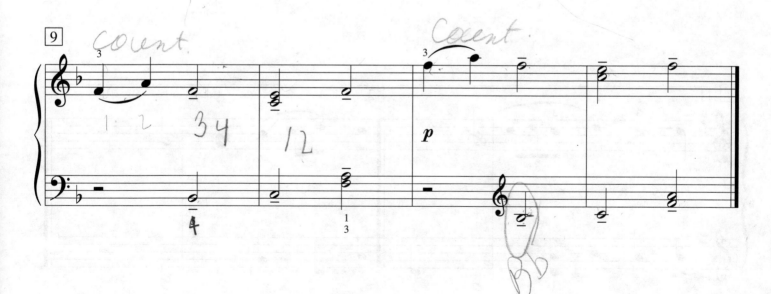

A SONG / UNE CHANSON

Erkki Melartin
(1875 - 1937)

LIST B

Andantino ♩ = 63 - 69

MIST / LA BRUME

Clifford Poole
(1916 -   )

Andante ♩ = 108

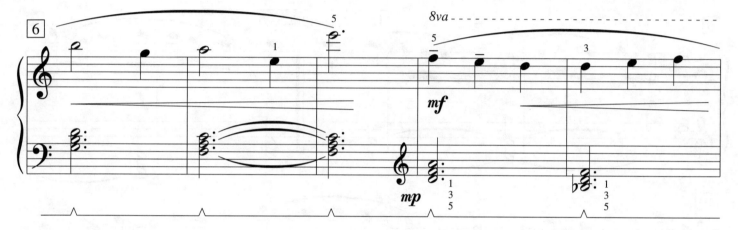

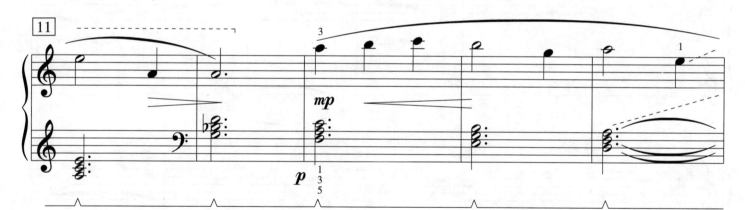

THE JOLLY FIDDLER / LE JOYEUX VIOLONEUX
Op. 41, No. 5

LIST B

Grigori Frid
(1915 -   )

Lively / Vivant ♩ = 96 - 112

Source: *Pedagogical Repertoire, First Year / Répertoire pédagogique, l'année première*
First edited in *Piano Pieces Album,* by Grigori Frid, 1961, "Soviet Composer," Moscow. Used by permission of the composer.

THE BEAR IN THE FOREST / L'OURS DANS LA FORÊT
Op. 11, No. 6

LIST B

Vladimir Blok
(1934 -   )

Slowly / Lentement ♩ = 56 - 60

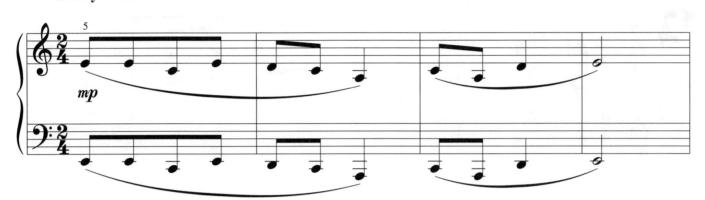

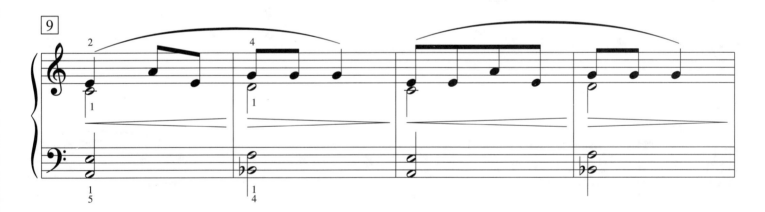

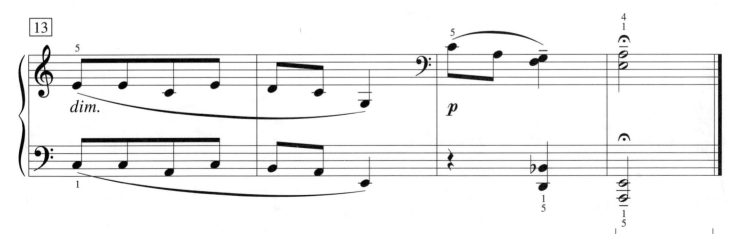

Source: *Pedagogical Repertoire, First Year / Répertoire pédagogique, l'année première*
Published 1980 by Muzyka Moscow. Used by permission of the composer.

MARCHING TRUMPETS /
LES TROMPETTES EN MARCHE

LIST B

Boris Berlin
(1907 -   )

In March Time /
Tempo de marche ♩ = 126 - 132

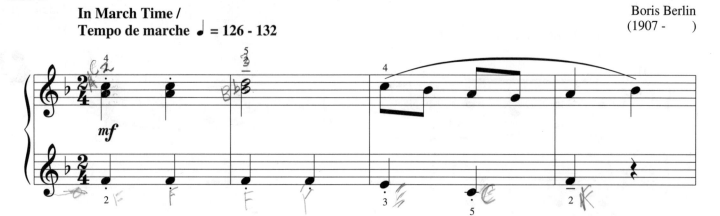

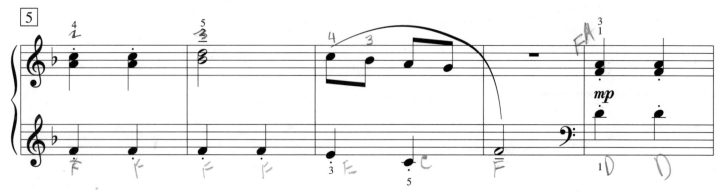

FAIRY TALE / CONTE DE FÉE

LIST B

Alexandr T. Grechaninov
(1864 - 1956)

Moderato ♩ = 92 -104

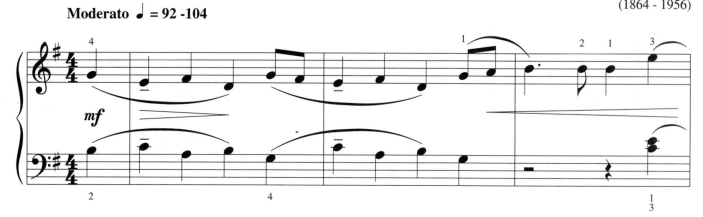

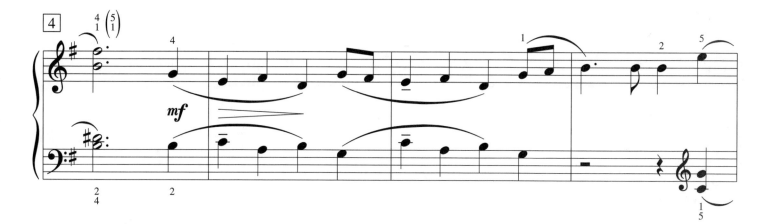

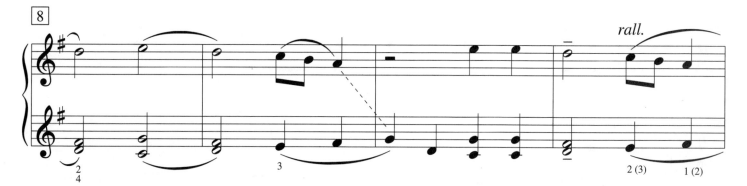

Source: *Children's Album,* Op. 98, No. 1 / *Livre des enfants,* op. 98, n° 1 (1923)
© 1937 B. Schott's Soehne, Mainz. © renewed Schott & Co. Ltd., London. Used by permission of European American Music Distributors Corporation, sole U.S. and Canadian agent for Schott & Co. Ltd., London.

BABY BIRDS / LES OISELETS

LIST B

Vladislav Shut'
(1941 -   )

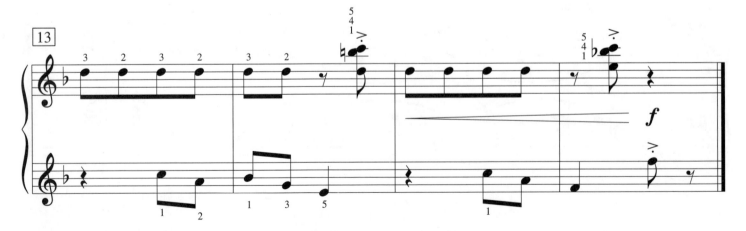

Source: *The Young Pianist*, rev. ed. / *Le jeune pianiste*, ed. rev.
© Copyright 1975 Soviet Composer, Moscow. Used by permission.

INVENTION NO. 1

Vyacheslav Volkov
(1904 - 1980)

LIST C

Andante ♩ = 60 - 69

Source: *The Young Pianist / Le jeune pianiste*
© Copyright 1970 Soviet Composer, Moscow. Reprinted by permission.

INVENTION NO. 2
Imitative Mirror-Movement / Imitation en miroir

Lajos Papp
(1935 -   )

LIST C

Allegro ♩ = 112 - 132

Source: *Starting the Piano / En commençant le piano*
© Copyright 1973 Editio Musica Budapest. Reprinted by permission.

INVENTION NO. 3
Leapfrog / Saute-mouton

Gordon A. McKinnon
(1952 -   )

LIST C

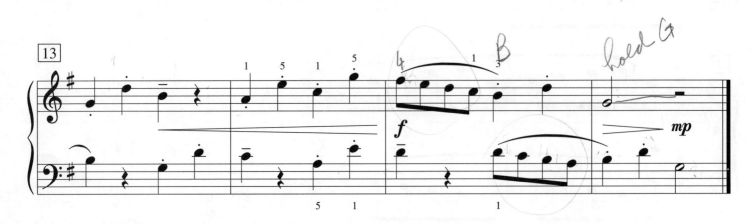

INVENTION NO. 4
Frère Jacques Stands On His Head /
Frère Jacques la tête en bas

LIST C

Clifford Poole
(1916 -   )

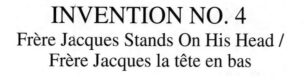

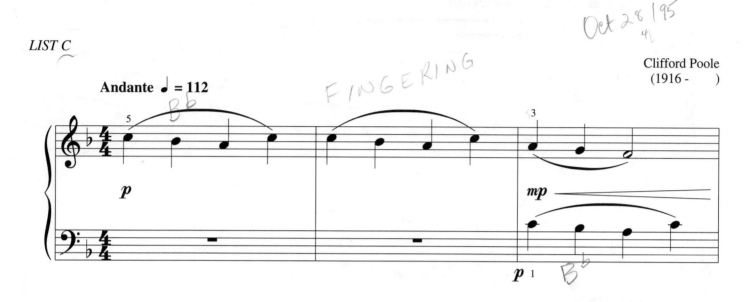

INVENTION NO. 5

LIST C

Andrew Markow
(1942 -   )

Andante cantabile ♩ = 69 - 80

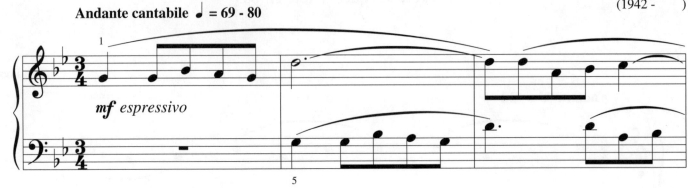

mf espressivo

dim.   *rit.*

INVENTION NO. 6
Waltz Canon / Valse canonique
Op. 14, No. 48

LIST C

Konrad Max Kunz
(1812 - 1875)

Lilting /
Rhythm doux et berçant ♩ = 112-132

mf

mf

Source: *200 Short Two-part Canons*, Op. 14 / *200 Petites pièces canoniques en deux parties*, op. 14